THE BEST OF
BRITAIN
Michael Leitch

Published by Chartwell Books Inc.
A Division of Book Sales Inc.
110 Enterprise Avenue
Secaucus, New Jersey 07094

Library of Congress Catalog Card Number 77 – 81862
ISBN 0 – 89009 – 147 – 1

Filmset in England by Filmtype Services, Scarborough
Printed in Spain by Mateu Cromo, Madrid

front endpapers
Hosts of golden daffodils still dance upon the
slopes of Rydal, in Cumbria, the home of
Lakeland poet William Wordsworth from
1813 until his death in 1850.

title spread
Compton Wynyates, Warwickshire: Tudor
splendour complete with secret staircases and
hiding-places.

contents spread
Fishing boats drawn up on the shingle bank at
Hastings in East Sussex. One of the Cinque
Ports, its harbour is fast disappearing before
the encroachments of the English Channel.

back endpapers
The sun sets over Stonehenge, Wiltshire, as it
has done for 4,500 years or more.

Contents

Introduction 8

Map 9

London 10

The South 18
including Hampton Court 24-5
Windsor 26-7
Brighton 28-9
Canterbury 30-1

The Flatlands 32
including Cambridge 36-7

Land of Farmers 38

The West 42
including Bath 48-9

Wales 50

Country Life 54

The Midlands 58
including Oxford 64-5
Stratford-upon-Avon 66-7

The North 68
including York 76-7

Mysterious Britain 78

Scotland 82
including Edinburgh 90-1

Acknowledgments 93

Introduction

To choose as a title *The Best of Britain* may seem a bit provocative.
But our intention has been to present a synoptic view that reproduces
all the finest and most characteristic visual flavours of the British
countryside. The main chapters of the book cover eight regions,
counting London, and within those chapters are spotlighted ten
regional centres. In order of appearance these are Windsor, Hampton
Court, Brighton, Canterbury, Cambridge, Bath, Oxford, Stratford,
York, and Edinburgh. Added to the eight main regional chapters are
three nationwide ones – on farming, country life, and mysterious
Britain – that are included as a way of reinforcing the human aspects
of our subject. All through the book we have tried to people our landscapes, to show the countryside as it is lived in, but in the regional
chapters the scenery itself has generally been given priority.

Selecting the pictures was a long process that involved choosing
approximately 120 from a thick pile of envelopes that in the beginning
must have held more than 2,000 technically acceptable transparencies.
The task, shared between four people – author, editor, designer, and
picture researcher – was spread over several extended sessions. The
book by then had a fairly firm outline, and there were no memorable
disputes between us (except perhaps over the merits of the pig, who
eventually got in – see page 38). But, for all our harmony, the business
of selecting pictures is a very personal one, and it is probably fair to say
that, left to our individual devices, we would have chosen four fairly
different sets of photographs. Our biggest task was one of compression
– to eliminate pictures when we still had too many, and yet keep a good
balance. The selection of our Committee of Four you may judge for
yourself.

A word, finally, about the borders dividing one region from another.
Broadly, these follow present county divisions in a generally uncontro-
versial way – Wales is Wales, and Scotland is Scotland, etc. But we
found that deciding where to separate the West and the Midlands from
the South was not so straightforward. While most of Oxfordshire, for
example, can be placed in the Midlands without discomfort, the southern part of the county – the old north Berkshire – can only really belong
in the South. Similarly, south Buckinghamshire has been kept in the
South, and the border dividing West and South runs through the
middle of Dorset. People in Lyme Regis with close friends in Poole may
feel temporarily inconvenienced by this, but we hope they will come to
agree that it is for the best.

In assembling the book we have tried to build up a portrait that is at
once recognizable and fresh. It has been a pleasure to do. We hope it
will be a pleasure to look at and read.

An easy reference to the position of many of the places illustrated in the following pages and the sections in which they are to be found.

1 North Ronaldsay
2 The Storr
3 Eilean Donan
4 Alness
5 River Spey
6 Loch Quoich
7 Glencoe
8 Braemar
9 Loch Tulla
10 Glasgow
11 Queensferry
12 Edinburgh
13 Grey Mare's Tail
14 Caerlaverock Castle
15 Bamburgh Castle
16 Newcastle
17 Hadrian's Wall
18 Crummock Water
19 Ullswater
20 Keswick Carles
21 Langdale
22 Appleby
23 Blackpool
24 Huddersfield
25 Leeds
26 York
27 Caernarvon
28 Llyn Gwynant
29 Betws-y-Coed
30 Llangollen
31 Cenarth
32 Ammanford
33 Stoke-on-Trent
34 Ironbridge
35 Belvoir
36 Loughborough
37 Foxton Locks
38 Warwick

39 Stratford-upon-Avon
40 Pembridge
41 Symond's Yat
42 Chipping Campden
43 Broughton Castle
44 Oxford
45 Brancaster Staithe
46 Clay-next-the-Sea
47 King's Lynn
48 Ely
49 Cambridge
50 Lavenham
51 Kersey
52 Flatford Mill
53 Whitstable
54 Canterbury
55 Scotney Castle
56 Epsom
57 Hampton Court
58 Windsor & Eton
59 Beachy Head
60 Brighton
61 New Forest
62 Salisbury
63 Castle Combe
64 Bath
65 Wells
66 Cerne Abbas
67 Clovelly
68 Dartmoor
69 Mevagissey
70 Falmouth
71 Welcombe
72 North Poorton
73 Perranporth
74 Land's End

SCOTLAND

NORTH

WALES

MIDLANDS

FLATLANDS

LONDON

WEST

SOUTH

LONDON

The walled city of a Roman emperor
expands to become the most celebrated
Royal capital of the Western world.

In every nation one city is pre-eminent, the place selected for the ruler's traditional home. In Central London the marks of power – chiefly royal power – are everywhere visible. Here too we can trace the evolution of British civilization since Roman times, perceiving the new in terms of the old.

Today's buildings are far taller, and many more bridges straddle the river than did in the time of the Emperor Claudius, who founded Londinium in A.D. 43. He built just one bridge – adequate for a city on the Claudian scale, but hardly enough to bear the weight of present-day crowds. Imagine the scene at, say, London Bridge if tomorrow every commuter from the transpontine dormitories of South London had to queue to cross at that point. What a fountain of spontaneous indignation there would be, what a feast of that overripe wit and ferocious sarcasm that the Londoner reserves for his finer moments of adversity. It is as well that fourteen bridges and six Underground lines now make the crossing between Hammersmith and Tower Bridges.

A little over 200 years ago, however, there was still only one bridge. Up to the time of the Great Fire of 1666 London had expanded slowly since the departure of the Romans, and on the South Bank, except for the ancient borough of Southwark, there was little but open country. 'After dinner I sauntered in a pleasing humour to London Bridge,' wrote the diarist Boswell in 1763, 'viewed the Thames's silver expanse and the springy bosom of the surrounding fields.' In 1750 Westminster Bridge had been completed, but otherwise Boswell and his contemporaries would have crossed the water by ferry from one of the numerous stairs lining the banks.

The pattern of the modern city was begun shortly before the Norman Conquest, when Edward the Confessor built his Palace of Westminster, which remained the official royal residence until the reign of Henry VIII. Nevertheless, when William the Conqueror arrived in 1066, he found he required something altogether more substantial, and built the White Tower (the keep of the Tower of London) to serve as both palace and fortress. Later monarchs evidently agreed with William I's distrustful view of the British people, and extended and enhanced the Tower as a royal residence, which it continued intermittently to be until the reign of James I (1603–25). By then the more adventurous rulers had already moved outside the City walls to found palaces amid parks and fields. Henry VIII was born in the old medieval palace in Greenwich, and it was near there, apparently, that Sir Walter Raleigh

A band adds to the relaxed atmosphere of St James's Park, a popular lunchtime rendezvous of local office workers. On the right troopers of the Queen's Life Guard attend the Trooping of the Colour, held each year on the Horse Guards Parade in honour of the Queen's official birthday.

laid his cloak over the famous puddle for Queen Elizabeth I to walk on. (The present Palladian buildings were designed later, at the time of James I.) St James's Palace, another royal residence, was built by Henry VIII while his more grandiose plans for the Palace of Whitehall were carried out. This was to be a vast regal estate, of which the Banqueting House is the sole survivor; the other buildings were burnt down in 1698, whereupon St James's Palace became the official home

of the monarch, and remained so until 1861, when Buckingham Palace assumed the role which it has held ever since.

While over the centuries the monarchs may have moved about from palace to palace, they rarely strayed far or for long from the seat of government. Since the eleventh century this has always been associated with Westminster, where Edward the Confessor lived and where in 1097 William II built the superb Westminster Hall. The old Houses of Parliament, part of Edward's palace, were destroyed by fire in 1834 and shortly replaced by the present neo-Gothic building of Barry and Pugin. Also at Westminster is the marvellous Abbey, begun by Edward the Confessor and tirelessly added to by successive monarchs. Here kings and queens are crowned and royal marriages celebrated.

St Paul's Cathedral is London's greatest Christian edifice. Like so many of the capital's finest buildings, it was designed by Wren to replace an earlier structure destroyed in the Great Fire that consumed the greater part of the City. Today's rebuilt City is London's financial quarter, jealous of its historic connections as a trading centre and its close links with the Port and Pool of London.

The Great Fire, and the Plague of 1665, did more than anything to hasten the expansion of London, the well-to-do fleeing westwards to make a fresh start. Today the fashionable shops, theatres and restaurants fan out from Piccadilly Circus, into Covent Garden, Soho and Mayfair. But for outdoor relaxation we must turn again to the bequests of royalty – to the great parks and gardens that make urban life worth living. In the north is Regent's Park, named after the Prince Regent (later King George IV); to the west is the vast expanse of Hyde Park, opened to the public by James I, while around Buckingham Palace lie the rolling slopes of Charles II's Green Park, and the more intimate beauty of St James's Park, where Elizabeth I once staged tourneys. So all-pervading, in fact, is the presence of monarchy in the capital that London and Royal London often seem interchangeable terms.

below
Neo-Gothic splendour in Augustus Pugin's superb Chamber of the House of Lords. Every last detail was designed and supervised by Pugin, even the inkstands.

bottom
The Royal Hospital, Greenwich, laid out by Sir Christopher Wren. To left and right are the imposing towers of the Queen Mary and King William Blocks, and beyond, on the hill in Greenwich Park, stands the famous Observatory.

opposite
The magnificent Gothic nave of Westminster Abbey, 102 feet from pavement to vaulting; the latter is carried on dark piers of Purbeck marble.

William the Conqueror's White Tower, the keep of the Tower of London. Its fifteen-foot walls, though forbidding from the outside, helped insecure monarchs living inside to feel more at home.

below
Pike drill for the Yeomen of the Guard (or Beefeaters) at the Tower. Their red-and-yellow uniforms remain true to the original Tudor design.

bottom
Shimmering terraces by John Nash, built in the 1820s in Regent's Park.

15

An immaculate display of sea-food on Wally Herbert's Sunday morning stall in Bethnal Green in the East End.

left
A cluster of Pearly Kings and Queens and their families. Their astonishing outfits, which contain up to 30,000 mother-of-pearl buttons, belong to a tradition of ornamental costermonger suits and are worn on such special occasions as the annual Costermongers' Harvest Festival service, held at St Martin's in the Fields.

opposite
The Pool of London at dusk, looking back towards Tower Bridge and the City.

THE SOUTH

A tour of Britain's richer pastures,
watered by trout streams and
the undulating Thames.

From Wiltshire in the west to the shores of Kent, this is an almost uniformly soft, well-watered land, delineated by close hedgerows, woods and rivers and winding lanes. If the landscape seems tamer than some of its more northerly counterparts, this is because it has been more comprehensively trod, acre for acre, by the ploughhorse and the labourer who wrought and shaped it.

The wind may sing over the bleaker parts of Salisbury Plain, and up on the Ridgeway that runs from Aylesbury to Avebury a ghostly solitude may attend the long-distance walker, but the real pattern of the Southern landscape is better typified by the South Downs – gentle rolling hills that terminate in chalk cliffs and pebbled shores. Here is a rich agricultural land, famed for its plump tomatoes and plumper sheep, its low dwelling houses made of local flint, of warm orange brick, and white-painted timberboarding.

The western part of the region as a whole – that covered by the counties of Dorset, Wiltshire, Berkshire, Hampshire and the Isle of Wight – corresponds roughly to the old kingdom of Wessex, once ruled by Alfred the Great (871–901) who made the beautiful city of Winchester his capital. Many of the country towns have long pasts – Salisbury and Marlborough, Newbury and Abingdon – and exude a certain contentment as if recalling days when everything moved more slowly, when the farmpeople and shopkeepers in the photographic collections of the local museum actually stood about on the streets, gathering news and initiating debates.

To the east, two of the counties – Kent and Surrey – abut London and are thus Home Counties; another, Sussex, continues the southward direction of Surrey as far as the English Channel. They have in common the downland, and the east-west stretch of the Weald, once the home of a flourishing iron-founding industry, now returned to agricultural calm, its surface dotted with oast houses. Of the country towns, Chichester, Arundel, Farnham, Canterbury, and Tonbridge are representative of that Southern blend of prosperity-cum-charm. To the north of London, and culturally distinct from

the others, is the county of Hertfordshire; it is included here because its nature, though different, is still irredeemably Southern, as is that part of south Buckinghamshire which falls within our borderline. In this region are the Chiltern Hills, the fertile Hertfordshire cornfields, and some pleasant towns – Amersham, Chesham, and Hertford, and, of course, the Roman city of St Albans (Verulamium).

Once, the South was covered by a great primeval forest, thickly populated by wild boar and deer. The Anglo-Saxons set about clearing spaces for their villages and farmlands, and there are records of

A mare nibbles the grass beside her foal in the freedom of the New Forest. On the right is the elegant spire of Salisbury Cathedral, the tallest in England, seen from a simple Wiltshire meadow.

foresters who in a working life felled up to 30,000 trees. Under the Normans, large tracts were declared Royal Forest, and the inhabitants forbidden to kill game or fell trees; in effect the clock was turned back, and areas such as the New Forest merely reverted to wilderness. This dense forest flourishes today, and though circumscribed and crossed by many roads it can still offer pleasing surprises to the naturalist, who may well find rare plants, birds, and insects, while the famous golden-brown ponies run wild among the trees. Farther north, in Wiltshire, the Savernake Forest is a superb spread of oak, elm and beech, covering some 2,300 acres. Parts of it have been carefully arranged by man, such as the great beech avenues

that intersect the canopy, planted in the eighteenth century. In mid-Sussex, the Ashdown Forest is a survivor of primeval days, while in South Bucks the burnished glory of Burnham Beeches on an autumn day is one of the most memorable prospects of the Southern landscape.

Descending from Oxford, the Thames winds through a fertile valley towards London. Popular with boating holidaymakers – once they are accustomed to waiting in line at a persistence of lock gates – the river runs past tranquil meadows, villages and small towns that take on an increasingly opulent air – Wallingford to Pangbourne, around the north side of Reading (which, oddly, pays little heed to the Thames), and on to the spacious regatta town of Henley, bright with the heraldry of oarsmanship, and hospitable thanks to the excellent pubs of the local brewery. Beyond Henley is glamorous Marlow, beloved of the entertainment industry; from there the holiday boaters push on to the royal towns of Windsor and Hampton Court.

At its extreme edge the South meets the sea – the English Channel and the lower reaches of the North Sea. This rocky fringe of England is probably the most fought-over part of the land. Evidence of Britain's naval power can be traced along the length of the coast, from Portsmouth, where Nelson's flagship HMS *Victory* is on view, to Chatham, where she was built. In between are the famous Cinque Ports – Hastings, Romney, Hythe, Dover, and Sandwich (plus Winchelsea and Rye) – some now landlocked but once vital centres for the defence of medieval England. Today this coastline is more associated with pleasure or a happy retirement. In the west are the decorous resorts of Swanage and Bournemouth, separated by Poole's broad harbour. Out to sea is the Isle of Wight, containing many picturesque havens and three massive offshore rocks known as The Needles. In Sussex, Worthing, Eastbourne and Hastings exert a tranquil appeal; Brighton's is more rumbustious. In Kent the discerning traveller may sample the subtleties of Deal, the Dickens country in and around Rochester, and round off his journey with a plate of delicious oysters at Whitstable.

left
Heading for the estuary: brown-sailed Thames barges seek the wind during their annual race.

below left
An oyster restaurant in the old fishing port of Whitstable.

below right
A seafood buffet at Epsom Races, reflecting the inner fancies of the Derby Day punters.

bottom
A Fourth of June (Founder's Day) salute from the boys of Eton College. Dressed as eighteenth-century sailors, they parade on the river and call for 'Three cheers for the college and three cheers for the Queen'.

opposite, above
The strange beauty of Scotney Old Castle, a moated fourteenth-century tower near Lamberhurst in Kent.

opposite, below
A row of stone cottages beside the bridge over Bye Brook at Castle Combe in Wiltshire.

above
The tapering chalk cliff at Beachy Head, near Eastbourne, and the lighthouse.

Hampton Court

The stately Tudor palace of Henry VIII stands on the Thames a steamer's ride from Westminster. It contains the work of many periods but its front facade states its origins. In about 1520 building was begun to the instructions of Cardinal Wolsey; then Henry VIII saw the results, coveted what he saw, and persuaded the Cardinal to make the Palace over to him. He added wings to the west front, and built the Great Hall and the Chapel. The eastern end of the palace was later demolished by Sir Christopher Wren, who redesigned the garden facade and Fountain Court. All around the Palace are river and gardens, the Thames enclosing on two sides the handsome park with its formal lawns, avenues, and Long Water, a narrow artificial lake.

Approaching from the west the visitor passes through the Trophy Gates and across an outer court to the bridge that crosses the moat (this is the view shown on the facing page). The first inner court is Base Court, built during Cardinal Wolsey's tenure. At the far end is the beautiful Ann Boleyn Gateway (see right) that leads into Clock Court. From here steps lead up to Henry VIII's Great Hall, a long banqueting room much taller than it is wide, and crowned with Joseph Needham's superb hammerbeam roof. The Great Hall also contains a fine oriel window, especially impressive when viewed from the exterior in Clock Court. Also of Tudor vintage is the Chapel, with its Renaissance altar-piece. Sir Christopher Wren's contributions complete the Palace buildings.

Hampton Court Palace is associated with two parks, its own and Bushy Park, a 1,000-acre spread lying to the north, on the other side of a road that cuts across to Kingston Bridge. In Bushy Park is the majestic Chestnut Avenue, one mile long, laid out by Wren and descending towards the Palace as far as the Diana Fountain. Nearby, on the Hampton Court Park side of the road, is the Maze, while on the south side of the Palace, next to the river, are the Privy Garden, featuring splendid ornamental iron gates by Tijou, and the Pond Garden. Here too is the prolific Great Vine, planted in its present position in 1769, since when it has swelled to a magnificent circumference of seven feet.

above
At the entrance to Clock Court is Ann Boleyn's Gateway, surmounted by the astronomical clock that Nicholas Oursian made for Henry VIII.

opposite, above
The front facade of the Palace, seen from across the moat, with its angle turrets, oriel window and terracotta medallions of Roman emperors.

opposite, below
The finely trained branches of the Great Vine, planted in 1769 and still producing a rich annual crop of black grapes.

Windsor

The greatest attraction of this pleasant riverside town is the Castle, the largest in the world still inhabited by royalty. It was begun by William the Conqueror, who built the central motte or mound and a wooden fortress that is mentioned in the *Domesday Book* (1084). The first stone buildings – the shell-keep (the present Round Tower), flanked by two elongated baileys or walled surrounds – were erected in about 1170, since when various monarchs have added some parts and restored others. The principal entrance is through the Henry VIII gateway (in the lower right-hand corner in the photograph), which gives on to the Lower Ward and St George's Chapel, a superb Perpendicular building completed in 1511. Here the Knights of the Order of the Garter are invested at an annual ceremony, and the banners of the knights are displayed in the choir. Many kings and queens are buried in the Chapel, the latest being King George VI, who died in 1952.

On the far side of the Round Tower, in the Upper Ward, are the state apartments. Here the Royal Family spend part of the year, in a private section of the East Front.

Sixteen state rooms are usually open to the public, and these are outstandingly rich in paintings and furniture, with ceilings by Verrio, carvings by Grinling Gibbons, Gobelins tapestries, and many Dutch Old Master pictures.

Nearby is the Home Park, a 400-acre expanse which contains the Royal Mausoleum where Queen Victoria and Prince Albert are buried (this is seldom open to the public). Beyond is the vast Windsor Great Park, with some fine formal gardens, and the safari park on neighbouring St Leonard's Hill.

The town of Windsor offers pleasant views of the river and many picturesque corners, as well as some attractive Georgian and Victorian houses. Across the river is Eton, its narrow High Street leading to Eton College, probably the most famous school in the world. It was founded in 1440 by Henry VI, who also founded King's College, Cambridge, and like that college it has a remarkably fine chapel that flanks one side of the main quadrangle. Tradition dies hard at Eton, and tail coats and striped trousers are still worn for morning school.

opposite

The Queen's Audience Chamber, with billowing ceiling decorations by Verrio; the walls are hung with tapestries from the famous Gobelins factory in Paris.

below

In this aerial view can be seen the plan of the present Castle and how it grew outwards from the central motte or mound; on the lower slope in the foreground is St George's Chapel.

Brighton

It would be hard not to like Brighton. Salt from the sea encrusts her buildings and erodes her paintwork, and she seems forever in need of running repairs – judicious patch-ups before the next trainloads from London descend the hill, dispersing among her alleyways to look in wonder at the prices on the antiques, populating the capacious bars, and, ultimately, striking out for the 'brine'. All are soon absorbed, for Brighton is an expert at the pleasure business, offering day-trippers far more than they could ever hope to do in one day. And so they come back for more. 'Blimey, not you again!' Brighton seems to say, with a grin. 'Come down for a bracer, have you?'

Brighton is, typically, the Londoner's seaside. Its history as a holiday centre began when an eighteenth-century physician, Dr Richard Russell, decided that sea-bathing, sea air, and moderate doses of sea water were good for the health, never more so than when taken at the fishing village of Brighthelmstone. Soon the well-to-do were directing their carriages there in large numbers. Royal patronage followed, the Prince Regent (who became King George IV) setting in motion the construction of Brighton's beautiful Regency terraces. For himself, he commissioned a Classical residence, its interior decorated in the 'Chinese style', later transformed into John Nash's amazing Royal Pavilion, with its bunch-of-onion domes and slender minarets.

Brighton's secret may be that she has assembled such a barrage of strange and unexpected things. The Lanes combine the eccentricities of an old quarter with sophisticated shops and bright piazzas. The Palace Pier is less surprising, but if you like piers or have children who do, you will find it a very fine one, more varied and exciting than its immediate rivals along the South Coast. Nearby are the splendid Aquarium-Dolphinarium complex, Louis Tussaud's Waxworks – with a most grisly tableau in its front window – and the terminus of Volk's Electric Railway, from where, every seven minutes in season, ancient electric trains clatter sedately towards Black Rock and the grey hulk of the emergent Marina.

Water sports in the shallows beside the pier. Although Dr Russell, who 'discovered' Brighton, advocated drinking the sea water, this might bring upsetting results today.

opposite
A viridescent wing of Nash's onion-domed Royal Pavilion, built in the Moghul style for the Prince Regent.

below
Elegant ironwork decorates the bow-fronted facades of Regency Square, one of the developments inspired by the Prince Regent's patronage of Brighton.

Canterbury

If Geoffrey Chaucer were just starting to compose his *Canterbury Tales*, he might include among his pilgrims a long-distance lorry driver, and perhaps recast the Wife of Bath as the Wife of Boulogne, an *expérimentée* French housewife heading to Canterbury for an orgy of *le shopping*. But no radical changes would be called for (save only that the modern visitor tends to be a touristic rather than a religious pilgrim). The fourteenth century has worn well in Canterbury, as the city walls, the apparently indestructible keep of the old castle, and the West Gate bear witness. Such changes as have occurred have done little to alter its essential spirit.

The Cathedral remains the dominant attraction and force, a reassuring monument to the vicissitudes of Christianity in England. The city became the focal point of the English Church shortly after St Augustine's arrival in the late sixth century. There are no remains of the cathedral that he built; the ravages of later Danish invaders were virtually total. The present building replaces one destroyed by fire in the late eleventh century. It was built by Lanfranc, the first Norman archbishop, since when it has been much changed and added to. The Bell Harry Tower, containing a superb fan-vaulted ceiling, is the central feature of the Cathedral and, from the exterior, the most arresting. The stained glass windows at Canterbury are of incalculable worth: the medieval work includes the South Window, and the Miracle Windows in the Trinity Chapel. The crypt is large and imposing, with tall pillars and a vaulted roof. Nearby, and of great beauty, are the cloisters. These belong to the adjoining Benedictine monastery.

Around the town the visitor will see many other fine churches and the ruins of St Augustine's Abbey. At The Weavers is an exhibition commemorating the craftsmanship of the many Flemish and Huguenot refugees who settled in the city; the houses here overlook the River Stour, a pleasant stream that winds through and beneath the city. For the literary pilgrim, finally, there is the monument to Christopher Marlowe in Dane John Gardens, erected on a prehistoric mound.

The religious face of Canterbury is here represented by Old Testament figures in stained glass, below, and the stillness and lofty symmetry, opposite, of the cloisters in the Benedictine monastery adjoining the Cathedral. At the bottom of the page, the River Stour glides beneath The Weavers, a collection of Tudor houses.

THE FLATLANDS

Marsh, fen and broad surround a heartland
still rich in rural crafts and practices.

From the borders of Humberside to the Thames estuary lies a massive swathe of predominantly low-lying agricultural land, remote for most of its extent, dramatic with steep skies, battered by east winds that sweep in from the sea. As somewhere to live and work, these Flatlands have always been prized for their unchanging nature. Townees exit coughing from London to settle there, attracted just as were Flemish weavers in the Middle Ages, and Huguenots on the run from religious persecutors.

Lincoln is the northernmost capital of our region. The old city stands on a hilltop and was settled by the Romans, who called it Lindum Colonia; the beautiful cathedral is the third largest in England and houses the finest contemporary copy of the Magna Carta. Eastwards are two bracing resorts, Mablethorpe and Skegness.

The Lincolnshire marshes and fens make excellent farmland, the former the home of Lincoln red cattle. The Romans began the work of draining the fens, planning and cutting dykes so that the waters could recede and leave behind a rich peat soil. Boston, at the heart of this country, was once a famous port, made rich by the wool trade with Flanders. From here Pilgrim Fathers set sail in 1608, arriving in New England twelve years later and founding the town of . . . Boston. Every Fourth of July the Lincolnshire town faithfully flies the Stars and Stripes. At Spalding, more than half of England's bulb crop is grown, and in season the fields of tulips, daffodils and hyacinths draw visitors from all over the world.

In northern Cambridgeshire and the adjoining parts of Norfolk, the Fenland continues – flat, mysterious because silent and foreign in its geometry of endless ditches and horizonless roads, intersecting mile after mile of vegetable fields. These alien characteristics penetrate south to Ely, and even beyond; but the city and cathedral are special, on their island, raised up from the daily round of dredging a living from the water-land. Indeed, before the Fens were drained in the seventeenth and eighteenth centuries, Ely was a true island, reachable only across special causeways or by boat. The cathedral is a

masterpiece of uplifting towers and turrets with, at the crossing, a unique octagonal lantern (see overleaf). Below the city, on the raised banks overlooking the torpid Ouse, the summer picnickers drowse and listen to the buzz of insects. South of Ely the land gently rises towards the grandeur of Cambridge, the county town and seat of one of the two oldest universities in Britain (see pages 36–7). To the east, in Suffolk, is Newmarket, perhaps the centre of the British horse-racing world. Here are the National Stud,

The bright-painted brick and flint Post Office at Brancaster Staithe, in northern Norfolk. On the right, also from that stretch of coast, is the windmill at Clay-next-the-Sea.

and the Headquarters of the Jockey Club; periodic horse sales fill this small East Anglian town to bursting.

North again to the edge of the Wash and the northern shores of Norfolk. King's Lynn is an excellent touring centre. Once a walled city and hub of the wool and cloth trades, as well as an agricultural town, it has two guildhalls and two market places, named Saturday and Tuesday. This part of the country is an outstanding area for studying bird life, especially wildfowl. Around the arc of the Norfolk coast are many attractive fishing villages and small resorts – Hunstanton, Wells-next-the-Sea, Stiffkey (where the cockles are called 'Stewkey Blues'), Blakeney, Sheringham, and Cromer. The last-named is more developed than the others,

with cliff gardens and a pier, from which the town's famous lifeboat is launched.

From this coastline the capital, Norwich, is reached via pleasant slumbering villages. It is an historic and bustling city, with a splendid Norman castle and cathedral whose spire is second only to that of Salisbury (see page 19); devotees of markets will enjoy the busy stalls here, their coloured covers recalling similar scenes in Flemish town squares. To the north-east of Norwich lie the Broads, an intriguing maze of streams and lakes, the flat landscape sprinkled with static windmills and the slow-moving sails of holiday boats; to the east and south-east are the substantial fishing ports of Great Yarmouth (also a cheerful resort), and Lowestoft.

Across the border the mellow charm of Suffolk waits in peaceful weaving villages and massive undulating fields, bigger now as a result of the sacrificial uprooting of many old hedgerows demanded by modern farming practice. Gainsborough and Constable celebrated Suffolk's leafy opulence, its rivers and church towers. The county's greatest town is Bury St Edmunds, the abbey ruins hinting at its celebrated past, its medieval and Georgian buildings offering a dozen pleasant walks.

The Flatlands reach to the fringes of London, but the traveller can enjoy the quiet of rural Essex within only a few minutes' drive of the capital. The rural villages around Dunmow, Finchingfield and the Hedinghams have been preserved with immaculate care, and the East Anglian craft of pargetting (decorative plasterwork) is to be admired on house and cottage exteriors throughout the county. To the east is Colchester. Once a Bronze Age settlement, it became a hub of Roman Britain and later flourished in the days before the cloth trade vanished to the North. Today its oyster business, initiated by the Romans, flourishes still. And so, finally, by sea to the Thames estuary, passing bouncy Clacton, sniffy Frinton, a batch of islands – Mersea and Foulness among them – and still more bouncy Southend, impressively endowed with the world's longest pier.

opposite, above left
The kaleidoscopic lines of the magnificent octagonal lantern in Ely Cathedral.

above left
Angled beams and vertical windows make a singular pattern on the front of this small medieval house in the Suffolk weaving village of Lavenham.

left
Flatford Mill, beside the Stour in Suffolk; made famous by the landscape painter John Constable, who was brought up there, it now belongs to the National Trust.

above
The square-built Customs House at King's Lynn in Norfolk, completed in 1683 by Henry Bell at a time when Wren's influence was at its height.

Cambridge

Many fine sights in this beautiful city may be viewed from two more or less parallel routes, one of which is a waterway. From Magdalene Bridge the River Cam (or Granta) flows past the backs of a succession of college buildings, and beneath some of the most picturesque small bridges in England. To the east, on the far side of these colleges, runs the second route, variously St John's Street, which merges with Trinity Street, which becomes King's Parade, and so on to Trumpington Street.

Near the top end of this undulating oblong the river is spanned by the barred and unglazed windows of the Bridge of Sighs, which connects the Third Court of St John's College with its New Court. The Cam winds on past Trinity College and its three-arched bridge to Clare Bridge, perhaps the most beautiful of all. Behind Clare College is Caius (pron. 'Keys') with its three gateways dedicated to Honour, Virtue and Humility. All the while the riverborne visitor can enjoy relaxing vistas of lawns, flowers and trees, the willows elegantly recurring.

One building that compels attention is the Gothic chapel of King's College. Begun in 1446 under the direction of Henry VI, it is a massive rectilinear structure with a turret at each corner, its roof topped by twenty-two pinnacles, eleven along each side. Passing along the Backs one arrives beside the wooden Mathematical Bridge at Queen's, whose Elizabethan intimacy of scale and warm brickwork contrast with King's grandeur.

On the roadway, in Trumpington Street, stands Peterhouse College, the university's first, founded in 1284 by the Bishop of Ely. On again, finally, to the Fitzwilliam Museum, which houses a superb collection of art and antiquities. This completes our tour of inner Cambridge, but space must also be found for some of the more recent institutions: New Hall, for example, the third women's college, founded in 1954, and Churchill College (1960), built to a similarly adventurous design. Both buildings underline the presence of a vigorous and up-to-date outlook – important at the present time, when the values of the older universities are no longer above scrutiny.

opposite, above
Poling, and doing nothing, in punts along the quiet Cam.

opposite, below
The harmonious seventeenth-century facade of Clare College, seen from the far side of Clare Bridge; the Chapel of King's is visible above the roof-line.

below
The dining hall of Trinity College, formerly King's Hall, re-founded in 1546 by Henry VIII, whose portrait hangs on the end wall.

LAND OF FARMERS

The working of the rural landscape:
a view of the industry that provides Britain
with meat, corn, vegetables and fruit,
and occupies four-fifths of the land area.

Almost the whole of lowland Britain has been brought under cultivation. This process began when farming peoples arrived in south-eastern England in about 2500 B.C. from the already fertile countries of the Middle East. With them in their boats they brought cattle, sheep, goats, pigs and seed corn. They hacked out clearings in the forests of Wessex and Sussex, and as their numbers grew they moved up into Norfolk and Lincolnshire, and eventually to Yorkshire and the Lowlands of Scotland. They were semi-nomadic, building wooden corrals to contain their cattle, but slaughtering them every autumn because they had no means of feeding them in large numbers throughout a British winter.

The Celts, who settled in Britain several centuries before the Romans, came from France and Belgium and were relatively advanced farmers. They had the ox-drawn plough, and used it to cultivate the land and establish farms and village communities. The Romans built cities and great roads to link them, but the work of clearing the country of its primeval forest did not begin in earnest until after they had gone. Gradually the Anglo-Saxons peeled back the dense forest and ploughed the heavy clay soil. They introduced a system of open-field cultivation, the land round a village being divided into big fields and subdivided into strips, each householder taking some of the best and some of the worst. From the air it is possible today to detect the patchwork patterns of those primitive fields, while in some places, for example near Banbury in Oxfordshire, the undulations created by the strip farms still clearly mark the land. In the centre of many villages there was a green, a common area on which grazing rights were shared. As for who was who in the social pecking order, at the bottom were the churls and above them were petty nobles and thanes or estate holders who owned the land. From this primitive structure has grown up the system that survives today in the country house and its manor farm, with land-owners cultivating their own farm with the help of hired labourers, and, if they were large landowners, renting portions of their properties to tenant farmers.

In time the common-field system was abandoned in favour of enclosures. Where this was done to encourage the keeping of large, profitable flocks of sheep, which a few men could look after, in place of arable farming which required a much larger work-force, there was great hardship as people were evicted from their homes and the amount of common and waste land was progressively reduced. By the nineteenth century most of lowland Britain was enclosed in generally small, hedged fields; the principal exceptions were in low-lying areas such as the

If the animal above were the National Pig, 30% of him would be used for bacon, and 70% for pork and sausages. On the right, a combine and tractor gather the harvest on Salisbury Plain, Wiltshire.

Fenlands which had recently been reclaimed from the sea, where the usual pattern was for larger, more regular lay-outs of farms and farm buildings. Techniques had advanced: farmers now drilled their corn seed instead of sowing it broad-cast, and grew turnips and swedes as winter feed for their cattle. The shapes of farm animals were changing, too, refined by selective breeding, while the machinery of the steam age was entering service; Carmichael's mechanical har-vester of 1820 was just one herald of things to come.

Concentration and efficiency are of necessity the gods of the present-day farmer. Britain is not so large that she

can hope to be wholly self-sufficient in food production. In fact, although this country produces 80% of its beef and all its main-crop potatoes, only just over half the total food requirement is home-grown. And so the land is increasingly subject to intensive methods of produc-tion, and to specialization. Instead of the old mixed farm, once the rule rather than the exception, today three-fifths of British farms concentrate mainly on dairying or beef cattle and sheep, one in six is a crop-ping farm and the rest specialize in pigs, poultry or horticulture, or are mixed farms. These various types are distributed all over Britain with, of course, different regional emphases. Most arable cropping farms will be found in Kent, the Flatlands, Humberside, and on the eastern side of the northern counties and the Scottish Lowlands. In the Fens, potatoes and vegetable farming predominate, and in the alluvial regions of the Thames, Humber, and south Lancashire. Dairy-ing, on the other hand, is for the most part contained in south-west Scotland, the west of England and south-west Wales; and sheep and cattle are raised on the hills and moors of Scotland, Wales, and north-ern and south-western England.

Farmland, as ever, has extraordinary visual beauty – the sweep of corn and mustard fields, and furrow-lines that pursue the contours of the ground; the clusters of farmhouses and outbuildings, the glare of tractor lights across open fields during night harvesting, and much, much more. And yet such scenes are of minor interest to the farmer. He is concerned more with his farm than with the scenery; a beautiful view will not buy him a new combine harvester (currently costing about £30,000). Although it would be false to assert that farmers are impervious to the beauties of the countryside, it may be reasonable to say that on their own patch they are mostly preoccupied with efficiency, and are content to leave rusti-city to others. For all that, some town dwellers may be surprised to learn that when they gaze from their cars at cows or cornfields, or hear the chugging of a tractor, they are observing the country's oldest and biggest open-air industry at work.

*Plough pattern in the rich earth
of the Eden Valley, Cumbria.*

THE WEST

A country shared by the Cornish
and the English, deeply carved by a
multiplicity of coves and combes drowsy
with sunshine and ancient legends.

From Bath to Land's End is nearly twice as far as from Bath to London. The West Country is remote, various, more difficult to comprehend than it might at first seem. In appearance it juts, like some great mechanical claw, far into the Atlantic, the pincers held open. But the presence of a claw, even a mechanical one, implies the presence of other limbs, of articulation, and a controlling 'brain'. The West Country, though, is not so easy to describe in such terms. Unlike the rest of England, where county shades into county without upheaval, the West is not all one.

The essential divide occurs along the River Tamar, which separates Devon and 'mainland England' from Cornwall. The Cornish people are of Celtic origin, and they remained a separate people until the ninth century. Their Brythonic Celtic language was generally spoken until about 1800, and survives today among a minority, its continued existence proof of a separate, living tradition.

It was near Gunnislake, just west of the Tamar, that in 838 King Egbert of Wessex overcame a combined force of Cornish and Vikings. From that date began the anglicization of Cornwall. The border river, the Tamar, makes an interesting study in itself. From the estuary at Saltash, near Plymouth, it winds due north across the moors to its source only a short way from the far coast at Morwenstow. (The latter was the parish of the eccentric Parson Hawker, who was once seen on a rock dressed as a mermaid, wearing a wig of seaweed and an oilskin over his legs, 'flashing the beams from a hand-mirror and singing in a strident falsetto'.)

Inland Cornwall is rocky and gaunt, once the centre of a thriving tin-mining industry, now virtually extinct; ruined towers mark its passing. Up on the moors stands Bodmin, since 1835 the county capital. Nearby is Brown Willy, at 1,375 feet the highest point in Cornwall.

Around the coast are numberless rocky inlets and picturesque bays and harbours, variously used and avoided by generations of smugglers. In the north King Arthur's Tintagel attracts a stream of visitors, magnetized by the ruined castle on the headland. Port Isaac and Padstow, where once schooners were built, are pleasant

fishing villages, Newquay is larger and more popular, and Perranporth and St Agnes continue the pattern of quiet resorts with broad, sandy beaches. St Ives – port, town, resort, and artists' centre – is rich in legend also: to that coast came Ia, all the way from Ireland in a coracle to join her kinsfolk; there she erected a chapel, and gave her name to the place. Around the head is Land's End, the most westerly point in Britain; across the sea are the Isles of Scilly, a haven of flower and bulb growers. Penzance and Newlyn are towns of some size; in between is the island charm of St Michael's Mount, where a

A purposeful ship's figurehead stands outside a chandler's shop in Upton Slip, Falmouth, Cornwall. On the right is a steep cobbled lane in Clovelly, Devon, where cars are banned and donkeys are the traditional means of transport.

Benedictine chapel became a fortress. Along the southern coast the visual charm continues, the road to Plymouth alive with ports and beaches – Mevagissey, Fowey, Polperro, and so on into Devon.

From here as far as Lyme Regis in Dorset is a succession of picturesque smugglers' bays, the stone a little warmer than Cornwall's, the scenery more verdant. Salcombe, on the Kingsbridge estuary, is especially attractive for sailing holidays, while Brixham is a busy fishing centre. Torquay is different, a grand resort, its palm trees and baronial hotels much photographed. Upriver from Exmouth is the county town, Exeter, graced

with a magnificent cathedral, a guild-hall that may be the oldest municipal building in England, and, with Taunton's, one of the two most important livestock markets in the West. Along the coast Lyme Regis, a medieval port, was well loved by Jane Austen, who walked the walls of the Cobb, the old harbour, and mounted the steep main street, where the shops are. To the east is Chesil Bank, an extraordinary offshore bank of shingle, a geological wonder; and nearby is Abbotsbury swannery.

The interior of Devon is dominated by the vast granite upland of Dartmoor, a lonely and sometimes eerie place, rich in burial mounds, stone circles, and mysterious piles of stones, some no doubt inspired by the natural shapes of the tors, the outcrops of granite found at the summit of certain hills. Chagford is a pleasant small town from which to explore the Moor. But, when in the northern part, beware the Army, which uses it for shooting practice. To the east is the well-watered moorland of Exmoor, extending into mellow Somerset. Here red deer and wild ponies flourish, gazed on by ever-curious buzzards.

The northern coastline runs from the Cornish border up beside the Atlantic and the Bristol Channel. It, too, is liberally provided with resorts, some, like Clovelly, exerting the appeal of the miniature, others, like Ilfracombe and Weston-super-Mare, presenting a larger canvas to admire. Bristol is a mercantile centre, a city-port well founded in the wine and tobacco trades, and with many fine buildings, the most spectacular being Brunel's Clifton Suspension Bridge (1864), spanning the Avon Gorge. Inland is the near-perfect city of Bath (see pages 48–9) and Wells, with its marvellous medieval cathedral. A mention, at the last, of Glastonbury, its ruined abbey and tor, where Joseph of Arimathea is said to have buried the chalice used at the Last Supper, and where his staff, buried in the ground, took root as a flowering thorn tree. For other visitors it is the place where King Arthur and Queen Guinevere lie buried. Glastonbury makes an apt symbol of the West – a land of diversity, legend and dream.

Border country: Britain meets
the Atlantic at Land's End, the
vertically structured granite cliffs
descending sixty feet to the ocean.

below
*Fishing and pleasure boats in
the harbour at Mevagissey,
Cornwall, once a centre of the
pilchard trade. Steeply banked
cottages crowd the harbour.*

bottom
*A fleet of sand yachts at Perran-
porth in Cornwall, a former
tin-mining village, where firm
beach extends for almost three
miles.*

below
A sheep, perhaps injudiciously skylined, on Crockern Tor, Dartmoor. In the twelfth century a powerful union of freelance tin miners held their so-called 'parliament' at this deserted spot.

bottom
A cottager at Welcombe, Devon, with his scythe, a useful implement for taming the uneven slopes of the 'combes' or valleys of that county.

opposite
Stone stairs leading to the Chapter House in Wells Cathedral, Somerset. The cathedral was begun in about 1180 and is one of the West Country's outstanding medieval buildings.

Bath

Few English towns can announce themselves so evocatively as . . . Bath. Battle, in Sussex, has this immediate, self-descriptive quality, as have others such as Bakewell, Coalville, and Land's End. Go to each and you can be certain of what you will find. But Bath is more forceful, more personal, the sound perhaps reminding us subconsciously of our strong affinity with water, an echo of our pre-terrestrial days. At any rate we humans regularly fall under the magnetic influence of seashore and spa, and then set off to 'seek the waters'.

The hot springs are the core of Bath's existence. The Romans were the first to harness and channel them into special baths. Magical and medicinal powers were ascribed to these waters, and the Roman settlement became a city, Aquae Sulis ('Waters of Sulis') named after a local god. The name 'Bath' was bestowed by the Saxons, whose successors ignored the baths to the point of building over them, and they were not rediscovered until the late nineteenth century. However, knowledge of the local mineral waters and of their powers, especially in the treatment of rheumatism, was not lost, and several centuries later the genius of a school of Georgian architects gave Bath its present unique character and effectively reopened it to a fashionable clientele. The architects, John Wood the Elder, John Wood the Younger, Robert Adams, Thomas Baldwin and others, created a magnificently unified city of squares and terraces for all – and there were many of them – who wished to be *à la mode*. They used the warm yellow stone from the quarries at Combe Down nearby. Their superb buildings include Queen Square and the Circus, Royal Crescent, the Pulteney Bridge, which has shops on both sides, the Guildhall, and Bath Street.

The city of the Georgians has been fastidiously preserved, and little of great note has been added since. The elegant face of industry is represented by Brunel's railway station, a more picturesque aspect by the Kennet and Avon Canal, which begins at Bath. Outstanding among the modern attractions is the annual Bath Festival, founded in 1947 and keenly attended by lovers of music and drama.

above
Supreme elegance in The Circus, built by John Wood the Younger in 1754–8. It contains three sections of eleven houses, each with superimposed Tuscan, Ionic, and Corinthian orders.

right
The Great Roman Bath, open to the sky, eighty feet long and forty feet wide, the finest Roman remains in Britain. For centuries the Great Bath lay hidden: only in 1878, when leaks from the nearby King's Bath were being investigated, was it redis-covered and restored to view.

WALES

A view of wild Welsh mountains, lakes
and waterfalls, and a coastline guarded by
battlemented stone castles.

The Celts of Wales successfully resisted two waves of invasion that, by contrast, drastically altered the face of England. Although the Romans actually conquered the extreme north and south of Wales, they had scant influence on the rest of the country, and in due course withdrew. After they had next beaten back the advances of Offa of Mercia in the eighth century, the obdurately independent Celts then denied William the Conqueror possession of their land, at a time when he had entirely overrun the English. In fact they held out until the late thirteenth century, when Edward I at last overcame them. In the latter period the great Welsh heroes were Llewelyn ap Iorwerth and Llewelyn ap Gruffydd. A decisive weapon of the day, the longbow, was a Welsh invention: in 1182 an arrow fired by one of these deadly long-range launchers was said to have embedded itself four inches in a church door at Abergavenny; two more are reputed to have surprised a reconnoitring Norman cavalryman by pinning his legs to his mount. Small wonder, then, that the invaders from the east kept a respectful distance. For a long while after Edward I's conquest, revolts continued against English rule, and not until a Welsh dynasty, the Tudors, controlled the affairs of England did unity become a real possibility; legal union eventually came about in 1536.

Today's Principality of Wales is mainly an agricultural land. Half the population inhabits the industrial Glamorgans in the south, and a quarter can speak Welsh. Administratively the country is divided into the northern counties of Clwyd and Gwynedd, the central ones of Powys and Dyfed, and in the south those of Gwent, and West, Mid, and South Glamorgan.

In the north are the mountains, dominated by the Snowdon range containing the five peaks of Yr Wyddfa (the highest at 3,560 feet), Crib-y-Ddysgh, Crib Goch, Lliwedd, and Yr Aran. On a clear day the magnificent views extend to Cumbria and beyond the Isle of Man to Ireland. From the small town of Llanberis a pass climbs to more than 1,000 feet above sea level, and from the same town there is access to the mountains by cog-railway. To the east is Betwys-y-Coed, the 'chapel in the wood', meeting point of the beautiful

valleys of the Conway and the Llugwy, and from where three waterfalls may be seen – the Conway Falls, near Fairy Glen, the Swallow Falls (see overleaf), and the Pandy Falls. Snowdonia is richly provided with fast-moving streams, and lakes such as Llyn Padarn and Llyn Peris, near Llanberis, and Llyn Gwynant.

Along the northern coast are the resort towns of Prestatyn, Rhyl and Llandudno, and there are impressive medieval castles at Conway and Caernarvon equipped with the accoutrements of the romantic fortress – towers, battlements, and narrow firing slits in the stonework, and, at the

Guardian of an ancient skill – one of the coracle boatmen of Cenarth. These precarious-looking craft are used for salmon fishing on the River Teifi. On the right, a spectacular view across the mountains near Llangollen to Dinas Bran Castle.

latter, a gateway barred by four portcullises. Anglesey, the renowned 'mother of Wales' across the Menai Straits, can be reached by bridge from Bangor.

Dividing north Wales from the central areas is an arm that projects into the Irish Sea. On its southern coast are the attractive village of Abersoch, the resort of Pwllheli, Criccieth Castle and harbour, and Portmeirion. This last is an extraordinary place, having been entirely built in an Italianate style by the architect Clough Williams-Ellis, who wanted to create a unified and peaceful holiday village. A little way to the south is Harlech, dominated by a four-square castle built by Edward I to announce and maintain his authority in the newly

conquered land. Along the coast, in the south-west corner of Gwynedd, are Barmouth and Dolgellau, a splendid centre for anglers, and hikers attracted by the Precipice Walk and Cader Idris (the 'chair of Idris'), a mountain some 3,000 feet high. From nearby Tal-y-Llyn runs a railway operated by steam locomotives, including an original tank engine of 1865.

Midway down Cardigan Bay is the spacious resort of Aberystwyth, from where many visitors journey inland to the Devil's Bridge. This is the name given to the lowest of three bridges that cross the tumbling River Mynach as it falls down to the River Rheidol. Below Aberystwyth are the attractive stone seaside villages of Aberaeron and New Quay, while inland along the River Teifi are Cilgerran, with a ruined thirteenth-century castle, and Cenarth, one of the last homes of the coracle. These fascinating small craft are made by stretching a waterproof skin over an intricately crisscrossed frame of willow staves; of very shallow draught, they make a usefully unobtrusive lair for salmon fishers.

To the west of the busy port of Fishguard stands the village of St David's – and a cathedral. This is dedicated to the patron saint of Wales, who died in 601 after helping to convert Wales to Christianity. Pembroke and Carmarthen Bay have a number of imposing castles, but the pride of the southern coast is the natural beauty of the Gower peninsula, to the west of Swansea, where golden sands arc in a series of sweeping bays, some pitted with rock caves once used by smugglers. In the industrial heart of south Wales two perhaps unexpected pleasures are Cardiff Castle and Castle Coch, both of which were reconstructed in the nineteenth century by William Burges in an idiosyncratic version of Gothic Revival, with overtones of French and oriental influence; for romance in stone, they are quite the equals of Conway and Caernarvon. Less surprising, in conclusion, but still more memorable are the roofless ruins of Tintern Abbey, set in the dark, wooded hills of the Wye Valley, and where, wrote one enthusiast, 'the soul, pure and passionless, appears susceptible of that state of tranquillity, which is the perfection of every earthly wish'.

left
Even before Roman times there was a fortress at Caernarvon. The existing Castle was begun by Edward I in 1283, and restored at the beginning of the eighteenth century.

above
The rock-divided torrent of the River Llugwy pours over Swallow Falls, one of three fine waterfalls near Betwys-y-Coed.

top
Llyn Gwynant, near Pen-y-gwrd, one of the numerous lakes to be seen in the mountains of Snow-donia.

opposite, above
A bardic rite at the National Eisteddfod, held in Ammanford. The Eisteddfod is a festival of Welsh arts and crafts and is administered by the Gorsedd of Bards.

COUNTRY LIFE

Closer to the landscape and to each other,
country people remain wise in the
unsophisticated art of living together.

In a bumpy field, vacated, according to the usual evidence, only minutes before by a herd of very healthy cows, stands a trestle table. Behind it are a man and a woman. The sun is shining, and there are other tables in the field, and other less conventional pieces of furniture besides, but it is this table which attracts the eye. On it is a fading, hand-painted hardboard box, open at the top and about one foot high and two feet square. Inside the box a hardboard cylinder is glued to the baseboard. The cylinder is about eighteen inches in diameter and is divided around the circumference into ten numbered sections. At the base of each section is a small hole. 'Any more, please, for Mouse Roulette?' says the man politely every half minute or so. More people approach, and some pay the man 5p for a large wooden card. There are ten cards altogether, numbered 1 to 10. We back 9, then immediately see it is an unlikely choice, since Hole 9 is in a direct line with the sun, and probably will not attract the mouse. Eventually all ten cards are sold, and the man turns to a smaller box with a wiremesh top. The people holding cards press closer to the table. In the background a brass band plays selections from *Oliver*. The man removes the wire mesh, and, reaching inside, takes out a small cup which he places in the centre of the cylinder with the numbers. Now everyone can see the mouse.

It has a long nose for an ordinary grey mouse – possibly there is some shrew in it. At least fifteen pairs of eyes are on the mouse. It wrinkles its long nose and looks about it, but does not immediately move. There is a pause. The mouse blinks at the sun, then slowly climbs out of the cup and with indecipherable purpose walks round it once. Then it turns and approaches Hole 4 (on the far side from 9), pushes into the hole but stops halfway. One or two people begin to drift away from the table. We are tempted to do the same. 'It's not over yet,' says the man. 'He's changed his mind before and gone back.' But on this occasion the mouse is going to torment its spectators no longer; it carries on clean through the hole and into a wedge-shaped space

beyond. 'Number 4 it is,' says the man, scooping up the mouse and returning it to its box. 'Who has Card Number 4?' A boy holds up the winning card, and now the woman who has been standing beside the man comes into action for the first time, dipping her hand into the takings box to pay the boy.

We move on to try something else, or anyway to look at other people trying. There is a pleasant mixture of the familiar

Alert for a bargain, above, at the church fete in Pembridge, Herefordshire. On the right, the villagers of Thornby, Northamptonshire, celebrate Jubilee Year with a feast; on the wall hangs a picture of George V, whose marriage was commemorated in similar style.

and the unexpected: next to Mouse Roulette is the dustbin in which competitors must stand for Welly Throwing; beyond are Penalty Kicks and the Plant Stall. Elsewhere on offer are a Beer Tent, Aunt Sally, Bowl for a Pig, the Palmist, and Tossing the Straw Bale. In the distance, past some willows and across an apparently unfordable stream, a gymkhana is in progress. But there seems no way to approach it. So we don't bother, and buy more plants to compensate. 'The Glorious Tenth was blessed all afternoon

with glorious sunshine, and £297-43 was raised for the School Swimming Pool,' wrote the editor of the village newsletter in the following month's issue.

Fetes such as this one, held all over the country in their thousands, are indispensable to the economic and social life of villages and country towns. Regularly through the year there are coffee mornings, teas, jumble sales, bazaars, and competitions to raise money for this or that project: the church bell needs repairing, there is the Senior Citizens' Christmas Tea to pay for, suddenly the Village Hall will fall down unless it gets a new roof. During the school summer holidays there is usually a break, but for the rest of the year the village energetically follows its calendar of rituals.

The church and its services are an obvious focus of country life, no less important than they were in the Middle Ages. Through the Christian festivals, and other special days such as Remembrance Sunday by the war memorial, the presence of the church permeates the community. By bicycle or car, the vicar visits all he thinks would like to see him, and some he may feel less sure about. Less obtrusive is the occupant of the manor, or big house. No longer wielding the almost total power of previous occupants, and with staff reduced to perhaps a cook-housekeeper and gardener, he or she is nonetheless looked to for patronage and sponsorship. The local farmers – those rural industrialists encountered on page 38 – are usually figures of substance in the community, awarding privileges such as shooting rights, and giving turkeys for raffles (and now at last paying their labourers a living wage). The pub and the post office are the intelligence centres generally expected to know more and to share it out faster, tongues in the former lubricated with light and bitter – at weekends enough to fill a pair of wellington boots. The pub, too, may be the natural home of the cricket team, especially if the village green, that former grazing ground for cattle and sheep, is now the home of the Village XI . . . or X, or VII, depending on who feels available. Some things are best kept informal.

opposite
A carpenter turns out wooden hanging pieces in the Loughborough Bell Foundry, one of the last two remaining firms to make bells.

below left
A thatcher perches on a roof at North Poorton, Dorset. Increased interest in the countryside and its conservation has helped this once-dying trade to make a recovery.

below right
In the village pub – intelligence centre and scene of many-handed debates, laughter and reminiscence. The pub is also home ground for teams competing in local darts, cribbage, and billiards leagues – or whatever may be the local preference.

bottom
While the local 'old boys' fish, rabbit, and shoot a bit, the gentry goes hunting. Here the hunt is starting out from Belvoir Castle, Leicestershire, home of the Duke of Rutland.

THE MIDLANDS

Lush hill-lines travel north-west
from the Cotswolds, and form the wild side
of a region roofed by the slate-grey
Derbyshire peaks.

More than the others, this is a region of floating borders, a box-shaped zone of movable parts, its constitution not unlike a concertina's. Isolated, it has no coastline to speak of, and is vulnerable to encroachment on many sides – though not all: for Wales must stay behind its official dotted line; the Flatlands, too, are unlikely to dare lay claim to such stoutly Midlandish counties as Nottinghamshire, Leicestershire, and Northamptonshire. The same argument was used to safeguard Derbyshire from the North. But Cheshire was not so open-and-shut. One man's Nantwich is not necessarily another's. Crewe, on the other hand, just a goods train's length away. . . . surely no Northbound railway passenger could really feel, on being asked to change at Crewe, that he or she had even begun to arrive. We, at any rate, have kept Cheshire in the Midlands; not all things can be solved by latitude alone, but this, we hoped, was one that could. The south side was not easy, necessitating changes of a more revolutionary kind. Oxon and Bucks have had to suffer painful partition, leaving their lower extremities in the South.

That, then, is our Midland region (for a graphic representation, turn to page 9). It is a culturally diffuse collection of counties, and not all roads lead to Birmingham, the 'second city' (which nonetheless is centrally placed). The most spectacular and unspoilt countryside is to the west, from Gloucestershire up to Shropshire. There hill ranges and forests abound: the Cotswolds, the Forest of Dean, the Malvern Hills, the Clun Forest, the Long Mynd and Wenlock Edge. Various in character, they share a breadth and freedom that may surprise the newly arrived visitor. The southern part of this area was prosperous in the wool trade that flourished in the fourteenth and fifteenth centuries. The Cotswolds contain villages in plenty, and also a good number of small, neatly circumscribed towns, unified by the mellow grey stone of the buildings. Charlbury, Burford, Stow-on-the-Wold, Bourton-on-the-Water, Northleach . . . even in so limited a space it is tempting to describe something of them all; better, though, to stick to one, and that must be the so-called 'capital of the Cotswolds', Cirencester. This dignified grey town, once an important administrative centre of the Romans, has a superb lofty parish church, founded by the wool merchants, built in the Perpendicular style and decorated with fine medieval stained glass. Here too are some excellent Georgian buildings, and a valuable collection of Roman mosaics in the museum.

Surrounding the Cotswolds is a ring of famous towns and cities. To the east is Oxford, and to the north is Stratford-upon-Avon (both separately profiled, on pages 64–7); in between is the market centre of Banbury, where a Victorian market cross has replaced the famous

At the Gladstone Pottery Museum in Staffordshire, above, the old working methods of an early Victorian pottery factory may be seen and admired. On the right is a view down to the River Wye at Symonds Yat in Herefordshire.

original, torn down by the Puritans. On the far, or Welsh, side of the Cotswolds lies the inland port and cathedral city of Gloucester, and only ten miles away are the leafy avenues and Classical buildings of Cheltenham, one of the most elegant spa towns in Britain.

Across the River Severn are the hills of Herefordshire, cleft by the valley of the Wye, producing marvellous vantage points as at Symonds Yat (a gate, gap, or pass) illustrated on the right. The Wye marks one edge of the primeval Forest of Dean, rich in wildlife above-ground and in coal beneath, a private place, populated with small mining villages. Great Malvern, high in its own range of hills, also grew famous through its spa; today its bottled water is more universally appreciated. Worcester, well preserved with ancient streets and a fine cathedral, gives a broader hint of the industrial bustle lying to the north in the Birmingham belt that can be said to begin at Kidderminster, the carpet town, and extends eastwards to Coventry and north to Walsall. Within as well as on the fringes of this industrial powerhouse are many acres of open country, for example at Cannock Chase. Here a great oak forest once stood; now many forest rides remain and the rambler can quickly vanish among these and the pine and spruce planted by the Forestry Commission.

Cannock is on the edge of the Black Country, whose natural centre is Stoke-on-Trent, home of the great pottery firms such as Wedgwood, Spode, and Minton, a region also celebrated in the Five Towns novels of Arnold Bennett. To the north, Cheshire is largely an agricultural county, highlighted by spacious mansions and black-and-white houses such as Bramall Hall and Little Moreton Hall. Its ancient capital, Chester, is well preserved and dignified, its arcaded 'Rows' pleasant to wander in. To the east lie the magnificent Derbyshire peaks and moors at the foot of the Pennine chain. Buxton, the highest town in England, the Matlocks and Dovedale are prime centres in this steeply accented landscape. From Edale walkers set off to conquer the Pennine Way, a rugged path that runs 250 miles to the Scottish border.

Farther east, in Nottinghamshire and Leicestershire, the country subsides into a calmer plan, well hedged and wooded in the latter to provide more fox coverts and so give spice to the hunting. This gentle landscape continues south through Northamptonshire and beyond, broken here and there by the striking interventions of man, nowhere more so than at Stewartby, in Bedfordshire, where the narrow chimneys of the largest brickworks in the world form a contour extravagant enough to satisfy the dreams of even the maddest Elizabethan builder, and certainly upstage the polite symmetry of their near-neighbour, Woburn Abbey.

A Foden traction engine in a rally at Broughton Castle, Oxfordshire – a symbol of the nationally felt nostalgia for steam-driven days.

left
A marvel of the inland waterway system: Foxton Locks, in Leicestershire, where ten flights of locks assist the descent (or ascent) of the Grand Union Canal.

opposite
The beautiful 100-foot span of the cast-iron bridge that crosses the Severn at Coalbrookdale in Shropshire; it was opened in 1779.

61

above
Lord Leycester's Hospital in Warwick, transformed in 1571 into almshouses for old and disabled 'brethren'.

top
An elegant row of Cotswold stone houses at Chipping Camden, Gloucestershire, one of the northernmost Cotswold villages, in medieval times a centre of the wool trade.

right
Gentle fields of grass and poppies at Guilsborough, Northampton-shire.

Oxford

Oxford is one of the most satisfyingly unified of British cities. Present is fastidiously merged with past, the demands of commerce and transport carefully channelled. The harmony, dignity and golden-walled charm that prevail represent a high mark in British civilization.

By far the greater share of Oxford's treasures await the visitor to the quadrangles, chapels and gardens of the university's numerous colleges. Of these, some thirty overlook or are soon reached from either of two principal thoroughfares that depart north and eastwards from Carfax. These are respectively Cornmarket Street, which runs into Magdalen Street and the broader spaces of St Giles, and the High Street, curving and gently descending in favour of the eastbound cyclist as far as Magdalen Bridge.

On May morning, choristers at the top of Magdalen tower salute the arrival of summer with madrigals; in the distance, deer rise to their feet in the park, and on the River Cherwell the all-night punters roar and splash.

Back towards Carfax the colleges parade: University, Queen's and Brasenose, the latter flanking the entrance to Radcliffe Square and the magnificent domed Camera, one of the principal reading rooms of the Bodleian Library. On either

side of Radcliffe Square runs a maze of lanes and college quadrangles, all worth visiting, none more so than New College, its cloisters marvellously calming. Beyond, to the north, lies Broad Street, where the busts of Roman emperors define the outer walls of the Sheldonian Theatre. Across the road is Blackwell's famous bookshop, beyond are Exeter, Trinity and Balliol. Around the corner, in St Giles, is St John's College, its seventeenth-

century Canterbury Quadrangle now rivalled for interest by the grace and modernity of the Thomas White Quadrangle, opened in 1975. Old and new there co-exist in exemplary harmony. It has not always been so. In bygone days Oxford tended to view change with some ambivalence, typified by the slight shock on the face of the dodo in the University Museum, squinting from its glass case at a plastic model of the DNA molecule.

opposite, above

The silhouetted cyclist mounts the gentle slope of the High Street, here passing the entrance to Queen's College.

opposite, below

A broad view across Christ Church Meadows from the river to the College. On the left is a cluster of three notable buildings: from the left, the College Hall, Wren's Tom Tower, and the

spire of the College Chapel, which thanks to an order by Henry VIII, who transferred the See there, is also the Cathedral of Oxford.

below

An ornamental gateway at All Soul's College, founded in 1437. The College elects only eminent graduate fellows to its membership and has no undergraduates.

Stratford-upon-Avon

Were it not Shakespeare's town, Stratford would in any event give pleasure to the traveller in search of a pleasant old riverside town in the middle of England. Situated halfway between Birmingham and the deep Cotswolds, Stratford seems on good terms with the essential spirits of both: it has added some light industries to its traditional business as a market town, and remains a well-preserved and attractive place, with a basically medieval layout and many timber-framed houses.

For more than 400 years, however, Stratford has been unshakeably linked to the life, work and memory of William Shakespeare. He was born there in 1564, the son of a future bailiff of the town guild. He went to school in Stratford, bought a house, retired and died there. In 1769 the actor and theatrical entrepreneur David Garrick organized the first Shakespeare Festival at Stratford. The popularity of the project gradually grew, Shakespeare's birthplace was bought for the nation in 1847, and in 1879 the first Shakespeare Memorial Theatre was opened. This was destroyed by fire in 1926, but its successor more than flourishes today as the home of the world-famous Royal Shakespeare Company.

Detailed information about the many buildings linked with the poet may be obtained from the Shakespeare Birthplace Trust in Henley Street, which in fact overlooks the garden of the house where he was born. This has been carefully restored, and visitors can see the birthroom, the kitchen with its curious baby-minder shown below, and in a small museum upstairs is a desk from the Grammar School said to have been Shakespeare's. Other notable sites include the house at Wilmcote, four miles from Stratford, where Shakespeare's mother, then Mary Arden, lived before her marriage; Anne Hathaway's Cottage, the charming early home of the poet's wife, and New Place, the house that he bought after he had made his name in London. Only the foundations of the original building survive, but in another house close by is an Elizabethan museum, while the adjoining Knott and Great Gardens have tremendous charm. Shakespeare died in 1616, and is buried in Holy Trinity Church; his monument stands in the chancel there.

opposite
Shakespeare's birthplace : the kitchen of the house in Henley Street ; from the floor-to-ceiling device in the foreground pivots a wooden 'baby minder', which not only limited the travels of the smaller offspring in those days but also kept them away from the open fire.

below
The River Avon, a swan, and the distant spire of Holy Trinity Church situated in the Old Town. Here the poet was buried, and in the chancel is a monument erected shortly after his death.

THE NORTH

A robust and rocky land of grey-stone houses,
moors, lakes and dales, spanned by a Roman wall
and fringed by long sandy bays.

The photographs on these pages, though belonging to the rival cultures of White Rose and Red, may suggest one factor common to both: that it gets dark earlier in the North. So it does in the winter months. But given that the North has acquired a reputation for taciturn sombreness, exemplified by grey-stone buildings, granite-faced matriarchs, coalfields everywhere, townscapes blackened with the grime of heavy industry, excessive rainfall, etc., it might seem as though this great section of the country barely enjoyed natural daylight at all, let alone sunshine. Fortunately, although the Industrial Revolution has much to answer for in terms of localized blight, it would be hard to sustain such a gloomy view for long when faced with the real evidence.

Take Yorkshire. Occupying one-eighth of the area of England, it consists almost entirely of moors and dales, spacious, undulating, open to the sky. And much the same may be said of the other Northern counties, by which we mean those situated between the Scottish border and Merseyside, on the West Coast, and Humberside on the East. Topographically this describes a central spine of wild countryside, the Pennines, from which the land eventually descends on either side to the sea.

Both coastlines are freely sprinkled with holiday resorts, many of them strangely undervalued. For showbiz attack and a good time measured in decibels, there are no serious challengers to Blackpool's Golden Mile of summer shows, fun parks, bars, seafood stalls – and Tower. (No grim-faced matriarchs here.) Morecambe is lively, but on a smaller scale. Nearby is the more genteel town of Southport, a mecca for golfers, its vast level beach ideal for sand-yacht racing. Farther north, and up to the Solway Firth that separates England and Scotland, attractive coastal villages offer the visitor long wind-blown walks over turf and dune, and a varied bird life to observe – St Bees, for example, is a major breeding ground for puffins and guillemots – while the sea fisherman who stays near Maryport or Whitehaven should be well rewarded.

Inland, to the north of Morecambe, is the incomparable Lake District. The lakes, tarns and fells extend for some thirty miles, and many are within a short distance of the sea. Coniston Water is in the Furness peninsula, as is the southerly part of Lake Windermere. Farther north are the Langdale Pikes, Buttermere, Derwent Water and Ullswater. Much of the region became a National Park in 1951, which ensured the preservation of those dramatic landscapes that have inspired generations of fell-walkers, and countless literary figures, most notably the Lake Poets – Wordsworth, the Coleridges and Southey.

Through the engraved glass windows of the Jubilee Hotel, above, rises the clock tower of Leeds Town Hall. Opposite, in acid technicolour, are some of Blackpool's illuminations, the Tower in the background.

Across country to the north lie the remains of Hadrian's Wall. Built as a bastion against the marauding Picts, it runs from the Solway Firth to Wallsend, near Newcastle. The Wall was manned by garrisons up to 1,000 strong, and its turrets, forts and milecastles have yielded fascinating insights into Roman military and social life. At Vindolanda, near Haltwhistle, is the site of a Roman town, and other remains can be seen in Chesterholm Museum.

The greater part of Northumberland reaches away to the north of Hadrian's Wall as far as the Scottish border, where Berwick-upon-Tweed is the principal town. In between is a fine unspoiled land of large farms set in the steeply undulating Cheviot Hills. Along the coast are a number of charming fishing villages, some with a past history that their present modest aspects seem to belie. Holy Island (Lindisfarne) lies some three miles off the coast and can be reached on foot at low tide; here is a sixteenth-century castle and a Norman priory; to the south is Bamburgh Castle, once the main residence of the kings of Northumbria; south again are the picturesque fishing villages of Craster and Seahouses.

Newcastle is the heart of a fat industrial pocket, a multi-level city rising up from the north bank of the Tyne, its roots in shipbuilding and the shipping of coal from the surrounding fields, its new white buildings at dramatic variance with the blackish iron, stone and timberwork of earlier days. Descending the coast, with an indispensable detour to visit the fine cathedral city of Durham, we enter Yorkshire, more than once described as 'England's Texas'. Past the fishing port of Whitby lie the stately promenades of Scarborough, once a fashionable spa and still, like inland Harrogate, sought after as a refuge for retirement or a suitably dignified conference centre.

All around lie the moors and dales, sweeping tracts of well-watered, rocky hills, populated by hardy sheep; every few miles the rolling expanses are punctuated by a grey-stone moorland town. One such is Haworth, made famous by the extraordinary Brontë family, many of whose possessions have been reassembled in the parsonage that now serves as a museum and literary shrine. Larger, and scenically more arresting, are the towns of Richmond, at the entrance to Swaledale, and Skipton. Yorkshire is rich also in castles and ruined abbeys; the medieval monastery of Fountains Abbey, near Ripon, is a fine example of the latter, reputedly haunted. If, finally, one were to select just two country houses from all the North, these would be Castle Howard, near York, a vast Baroque palace designed by Sir John Vanbrugh, and Harewood House, near Leeds, an eighteenth-century mansion rich in Adam-designed rooms; its gardens were landscaped by Capability Brown, and there are aviaries in which exotic birds flutter and strut, like aristocrats in exile.

Reflections in Ullswater, one of the eastern-most lakes, second in size only to Windermere.

above
Blea Tarn Farm, Langdale. The farmhouse was known to Wordsworth, who used the dale in which it lies for a scene in his long philosophical poem, The Excursion.

top
Black Beck Tarn, Crummock Water, looking towards the northern end and the 2,800-ft swell of Grasmoor.

*Hadrian's Wall at Cuddy's
Crag. The wall is some 73 miles
long and extends from the Solway
Firth, just north of Carlisle, to
the appropriately named Wallsend,
near Newcastle.*

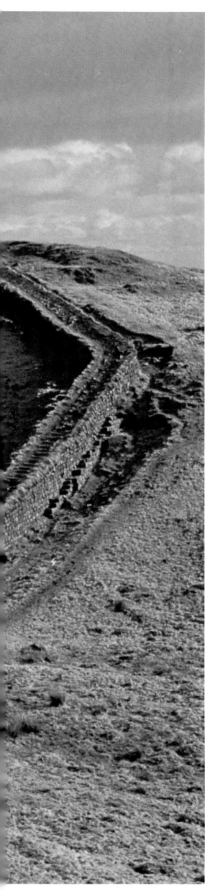

above right
Drystone walls straggle across the face of Stonesdale Moor, Yorkshire.

right
Appleby Horse Fair, held annually in June in the former county town of Westmorland.

Across the rippled sands Bamburgh Castle stands high over its village, since Norman times a landmark to North Sea shipping.

right
Solo practice for a bandsman in Huddersfield; to the listener, the sweet brass notes hang in the air with a special melancholy.

below right
The Tyne bridges at Newcastle, from the High Level down to the Swing Bridge, which almost noses the water.

York

It may seem odd, in view of the city's great age, and a name that suggests dominion over the whole vast county of Yorkshire, to find that the real York is a tranquil and unassuming place. This absence of metropolitanism cannot be blamed on the Romans, who built a fort at Eboracum in A.D. 71 and made it the headquarters for their military operations in northern Britain. Indeed, Constantine the Great was in 306 crowned emperor at this far-flung but strategically desirable city. Mementos of those great days have survived in the form of a tower, a statue of a legionary, and the hair of a Roman lady. But Constantine's true ambitions

York took on a more leisured existence. Civic buildings still abound, conveying an impression of confidence and privilege.

A source of endless fascination is the Castle Folk Museum, which displays period rooms and reconstructions of streets and daily life from Tudor to Edwardian times. A more recent addition is the National Railway Museum, its Great Hall containing two turntables and a wealth of historic locomotives. So varied, in fact, are the city's attractions, that it is a good idea for visitors to begin by going to St Mary's Heritage Centre, Castlegate, for a special presentation of York's history in sound and vision.

opposite
Part of the Shambles, the old butchers' quarter, where the steep houses lean inwards, funnelling the daylight.

below left
The Stonegate Devil, originally a printing house sign, crouches above the public way in one of York's narrow medieval streets.

below
The Minster seen from the fourteenth-century walls that encircle the city.

lay beside the Bosporus, and it is to later cultures that the city of York owes its present character.

The Minster is York's greatest treasure. Recently restored at a cost of £2 million, the original building was begun in the early thirteenth century, and was finished and consecrated in 1472. From the exterior, the abrupt magnitude of the Central Tower makes an unforgettable impression. Inside are superb stained glass windows, the best known being the Five Sisters and the Great East Window, believed to be the world's largest example of medieval coloured glass.

Other survivors of Old York include three guildhalls, seventeen pre-Reformation churches, and city walls that can be walked for some two and a half miles. These and several charming narrow streets such as the Shambles attest to a vigorous mercantile life that once made York the second city of all England. When the wool trade later moved away,

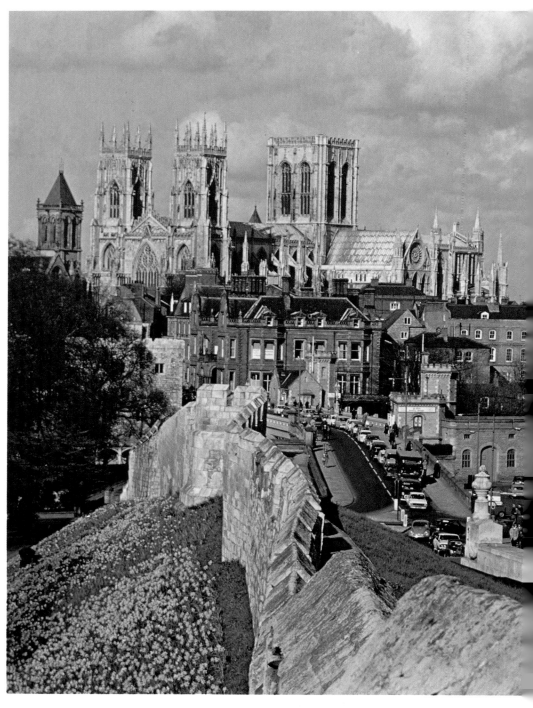

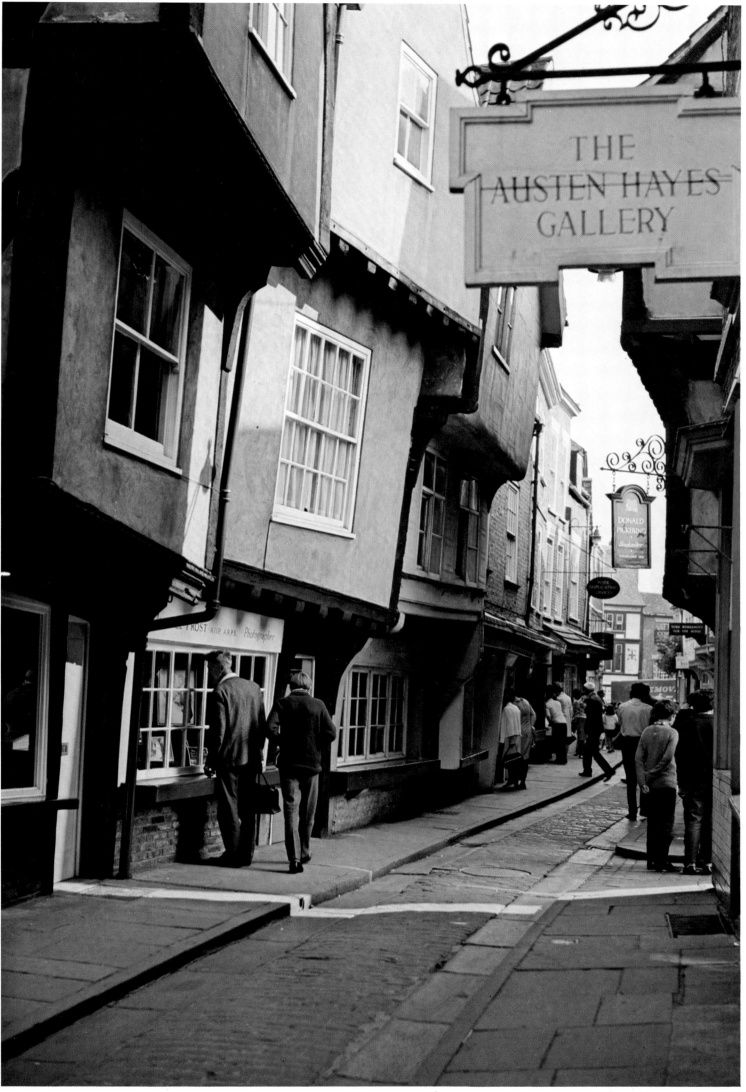

MYSTERIOUS BRITAIN

Stone circles, chalk figures and strange customs
remind us that the Pagan truths of long ago
are always near at hand.

In their efforts to understand the fearsome forces of nature and chance that defied ordinary explanation, the ancient Pagan priests devised supernatural systems. They built stone circles to measure and predict the movements of the Sun, Moon, and planets, invested them with godlike powers, and consecrated holy burial places where the respected dead would continue to work for them. They carved messages and figures on the hillsides, the better to signal their wishes to the gods, and enacted ceremonies to promote fertility and growth.

Today people are inclined to take a more sympathetic view than formerly of Pagan rituals and beliefs. We now perhaps accept that some things are inexplicable, and are more aware of problems of communication. In the same week that this piece was written, officials at the American space agency NASA had a fine argument over whether or not to include a photograph showing a full-frontal nude couple (man and woman) in a package of visual information about planet Earth which they proposed to dispatch to a distant star, some 40,000 years' flying time away. In the end they decided to put their faith in a set of diagrams describing human sex and reproduction. The artist(s) who carried out the Cerne Abbas giant (seen on the right) might have had a good laugh at the Americans' dilemma, and would probably have disagreed with their solution.

Our understanding of the early Pagans' repertoire of structures and images can never be complete. Research into British hill figures such as the Cerne Abbas giant reveals that they belong to many different periods, and most likely existed to perform a variety of functions. Those depicting phalluses seem to have had to do with spring and fertility. On the hillside above the Cerne Abbas man is an enclosure long associated with May Day and maypole ceremonies, and locally the giant was credited with being able to make a barren woman fertile if she slept the night on his body. Many other hill figures are of horses (possibly some double as dragons): these are often situated near an Iron Age fort, and may have been intended by the occupants to signal their presence

to gods or life forces in the sky; or they may be symbols of horse worship. Examples may be seen at Uffington, Oxfordshire, and near Westbury in Wiltshire.

Stranger still are the leys – the alignments which on a map will be found to link all manner of ancient sites such as burial grounds, standing stones, mounds and other structures of a sacred nature. The ley-lines were first discovered in the 1920s by Alfred Watkins, who told the story of his findings in a fascinating book, *The Old Straight Track*. As an example: if a straight line is drawn on an Ordnance Survey map from Stonehenge six miles

The Keswick Carles in Cumbria, above, may have been an assembly place for mourning the royal dead. In Dorset, right, people believed that a barren woman who slept the night on the body of the Cerne Abbas giant would be made fertile.

south to Clearway Ring, it will pass directly through the ancient earthwork of Old Sarum – site of a cathedral abandoned in the thirteenth century – *and* through the present cathedral, the siting of which was ordained by the Virgin in a vision to Bishop Poore.

In Watkins's view such leys were ancient trackways; it is possible, too, that they define lines of unseen cosmic energy, and therefore hold a greater religious significance. Ley-lines criss-cross the whole of Britain. To discover one can be most exhilarating, especially if it is near home. All that is needed is an Ordnance Survey map, on which alignments can be looked

for and traced, preferably on a transparent overlay. Once a ley has been found, the next step is to go out and walk it, testing the visibility of one point from the next, and perhaps, en route, discovering some ancient and forgotten marker stone in a hedge or beside a pathway. Thus may a new, mysterious landscape emerge.

A more dominating presence is that of the many standing stones and circles that are to be found all over Britain. Stonehenge is the most famous of these: the building of its great circles probably began before 2500 B.C., and was the work of the Beaker People. As Professor G. S. Hawkins's researches have revealed, the stones have been arranged to record an extraordinary number of alignments, noting the positions of the Sun and Moon throughout the year. One important function would have been to foretell eclipses, which instilled great fear into prehistoric cultures. The nearby circles of Avebury formed a gigantic open-air Sun temple: two avenues of stones stretch one and a half miles from a great circle, and one of these terminates in another large circle, called the Sanctuary. Variations elsewhere on these patterns include single stones, and groups forming cromlechs and quoits (vertical stones surmounted by a horizontal one). In Cornwall the Crick Stone near Morvah is an example of a dolmen or holed stone; these may have been thought to confer energy on anyone climbing through the hole.

Throughout the land the Pagan rites of spring are celebrated in ways familiar and less so. The antics of Morris dancers and maytime festivals may be generally understood; but there are many other activities whose meanings may seem obscure to a stranger. These would no doubt include the Burry man and the Pace-eggers, illustrated overleaf. Others might be the hobby horses, which parade in Padstow, Minehead, Abbots Bromley and elsewhere, grabbing at the local women and girls as they go (nothing too difficult here), and the various fire festivals, featuring bonfires, boat-burning, etc., which probably go back to pre-Christian worship of the Sun and fire, both of which were revered as life- and energy-giving forces.

A pace-egging play. This is an Easter ceremony, when eggs dyed in bright colours are rolled downhill to encourage fertility.

left
Morris dancers in Kersey, Suffolk; with sticks and bells they dance to help the plant world to germinate and flourish.

opposite
The ceremony of the Burry man in Queensferry, West Lothian. Each year a man is covered from head to toe in sticky burrs and led round the town; he is an ancient scapegoat for times when fishing was bad, and was ceremonially expelled in the hope that this would take away the community's bad luck.

SCOTLAND

Imperious mountains and the bright
waters of loch and salmon river
dominate these outer reaches
of the British Isles.

In devising a journey through Scotland it is tempting to move, as many holiday-makers do, from south to north on, say, the eastern side and then return from the farthest point along the west coast, visiting the islands en route. This method has the disadvantage, however, of cutting across rather than looking in turn at each of Scotland's three distinct regions, all of which have their own character. These are the Highlands, which lie to the north of a line running from Helensburgh to Stonehaven; the Central Lowlands, which descend to a line Girvan-Dunbar; and the Southern Uplands, a region of rounded hills that reaches south to the English border. There are also the Islands, most of which fall within Highland latitudes.

At the very top of the British Isles are two island groups that are rather more independent. The mainland of the north-ernmost group, the Shetlands, lies just over 100 miles from the Scottish coast and was for 600 years under Norse rule. On this bleak and largely treeless archipelago Shetland ponies, sheep and cattle are raised, and fishing and knitting are important industries (Fair Isle giving its name to a distinctive style). Separated from Scotland by the Pentland Firth are the Orkneys, the other group. Pomona is the main island, while North Ronaldsay, illustrated on the right, is one of the northern-most. Fishing and poultry farm-ing are the main occupations of the people, whose fore-fathers, like the Shetlanders', once lived under Norse rule, being finally pledged to Scotland in 1468.

Although there are some who would argue that only the upper mass of the Scottish mainland, that to the north of Glen Mor, can properly be called the Highlands, we take another view. The 'northern' argument fails, for one thing, to take into account the simple fact that the true home of whisky, or 'Highland dew' as it is universally known, is near the lower reaches of the River Spey, where most of the distilleries are located. Our division is also literally and geographi-cally more accurate, since it embraces all the mountain areas, or high lands, of the north – the North West Highlands *and* the Grampians.

It is a wild and exhilarating region. Immediately above the Highland border,

at Helensburgh, lies celebrated Loch Lomond. To the north is Glen Orchy, down which the River Orchy speeds on its way to Loch Awe; then Glencoe, with the Three Sisters, dour and massive peaks; from nearby Loch Leven the road up to Fort William runs beside mighty Ben Nevis, at 4,406 feet the highest mountain in the British Isles. To the east, as far as Ben Macdhui (4,296 feet) in the Cairn-gorms, lies one of Scotland's most striking stretches of country, the great mountains everywhere descending to long silent lochs, their deep sunlit blues contrasting with the greens, russets and purples of the

In the domain of whisky, above: the copper stills at Teaninich Distillery, Alness, where a Highland malt whisky is made. On the right is a portside view of fishing nets on North Ronaldsay in the Orkneys.

lower slopes surrounding them, and the darker granite shades of the peaks, the latter sometimes snow-covered. There is usually snow in abundance in the Cairn-gorms, centre of a burgeoning winter sports industry. The mountains make a fine setting also for the Braemar Games, best known of the Highland Gatherings, at which the customary athletic skills are tested along with regional events such as Scottish dancing and that ordeal of biceps and balance, tossing the caber.

Nearby is Balmoral Castle, used by generations of the Royal Family since it was built in 1853 by Queen Victoria. The Dee, which rises in the Cairngorms, runs nearby – and on to the sea at Aberdeen,

the granite city and centre on dry land of Britain's new oil industry.

The Grampians are separated from the North West Highlands by the long gash of Glen Mor and the Caledonian Canal. The middle section of this deep divide is occupied by Loch Ness, where the mon-ster is forever expected. On the far side, a great ladder of east-west lochs runs up the land, from Loch Eil to Loch Fannich. The western coastline is deeply scored, fjord-like, with other lochs. Out to sea is the Isle of Skye, largest of the Inner Hebrides, and beyond it are the Outer Isles – Lewis, Harris, North and South Uist, and Barra being the largest. Storno-way, on Lewis, is the chief town, a fishing port once active in the whaling trade. Less than 1,000 people in the Highlands now speak only Gaelic, the ancient language, although some 70,000 are still bilingual in Gaelic and English. At one time, before the Act of Union of 1707, the greatest opposition to the anglicization of Scotland came from this wild sector, but much of its political vigour has evaporated with the gradual decline in the population, faced with the increasingly uphill task of making a living from their small farms.

South, now, to the Central Lowlands, which enclose the principal cities of Edinburgh, the capital (see page 90) and the vaster sprawl of Glasgow, on the Clyde. The predominantly low lines of the surrounding country are broken by a range of volcanic hills, among them the Ochils, between the Firths of Forth and Tay, and the Pentland Hills. Some eighty per cent of the population lives in this sector, drawn by the comparative affluence offered by the coalfields and the dockyards. At Alloway, two miles from Ayr, Scotland's most famous poet, the anarchic Robert Burns, was born.

To the south, in the Southern Uplands, life is calmer again, sheep are grazed, and a more mixed type of farming is carried on closer to the English border. As ever, ruined castles like that of Caerlaverock (see overleaf) dot the coastline of a land rightly cautious in view of invasions prev-iously suffered at the hands of Picts, Irish Scots, Britons, and Angles (though other fortifications will be needed to keep out the present hordes anxious for a closer involvement in the oil bonanza).

above
The Library in Charles Rennie Mackintosh's Glasgow School of Art, probably the finest surviving Art Nouveau building in Scotland.

right
Caerlaverock Castle near Dumfries, whose moated shell retains corner turrets reminiscent of Scotney Old Castle in Kent (see page 22).

opposite, above
The Grey Mare's Tail, a spectacular strip of water that falls 200 feet from Tail Burn to Moffat Water.

opposite, below
A heavy-booted hammer thrower at the Games at Braemar, near Balmoral, most famous of the Highland Gatherings.

*The romantic Castle of Eilean
Donan, a stronghold of the
Mackenzies, strategically placed
at the junction of Lochs Alsh,
Long, and Duich.*

above right
Black Rock Cottage, a white-washed farmhouse, and the peak of Buachaille Etive Mor, near Oban.

right
Climactic moment for a salmon fisherman on the fast-flowing River Spey.

The rugged mountainside at Glencoe, the legendary birthplace of the poet Ossian, and scene of the massacre of the Macdonalds in 1692.

Edinburgh

Before the barrel of the cannon on Calton Hill, in the picture below, the city stands at bay. This panorama has captivated photographers since the beginnings of the art. George Washington Wilson, the Scottish pioneer photographer credited with taking the first 'instantaneous' views (in 1856), made several stereoscopic pictures that nicely point up the relief qualities of the scene. Of immediate interest, to the right of the cannon, is the circular 'Grecian' monument to Professor Dugald Stewart, the philosopher, which was copied from an original in Athens. Beyond the eye swings down to Princes Street, taking in the sturdy clock tower of the North British Hotel and alighting with greater interest on the pinnacles of the Scott Monument, dedicated to the novelist Sir Walter Scott. To the left, high on its rock, stands Edinburgh Castle, the foundation stone of the city, where King Malcolm III established his royal residence in 1128, and where, at one o'clock every day, a cannon booms the hour from the battlements.

Around the Castle there grew up the Old Town, which remained the true heart of Edinburgh until the eighteenth century, when the Nor' Loch around the Castle was drained and Princes Street Gardens were established in its place. The city then expanded in the shape of the Georgian New Town, here seen (with later additions) behind the Stewart Monument. From the Castle the Royal Mile extends parallel with Princes Street as far as the Palace of Holyroodhouse, official residence of the sovereign in Edinburgh, a French-style château with round towers that stands in a large park. Here is to be found the highest of Edinburgh's seven hills, an extinct volcano known as Arthur's Seat. Famous buildings flank the Royal Mile: St Giles's Cathedral, the High Kirk of Edinburgh; John Knox's House, and the jutting clock and turrets of Canongate Tolbooth, once a courthouse and prison and now a museum.

Each year this naturally civilized and pacific city celebrates its Festival, an international multi-arts feast attracting world-famous performers and a vigorous Fringe of adventurous amateurs on their way, they hope, up.

opposite
The floodlit splendour of the annual Military Tattoo, staged on the Esplanade in front of the Castle as part of the Festival.

above
A view across the city and, in particular, along Princes Street, from Calton Hill; the 'temple' on the right is the Dugald Stewart Monument.

top
White Horse Close in the old quarter near the Canongate; the latter forms part of the Royal Mile linking the Castle and the Palace of Holyroodhouse.

Acknowledgments

Aerofilms, Boreham Wood 26–7; John Bethell, St Albans contents page, title page, 12 top and bottom, 14–15, 19, 23, 24, 25 top and bottom, 36, 37, 44–5, 48, 51, 62 bottom; British Tourist Authority, London 21 upper right, 22 top, 28, 29 top and bottom, 34 top left, 35, 42, 48–9, 57 top left, 59, 62 top, 66, 73 top, 75 bottom, 80 bottom, 84–5, 85 bottom right, back endpapers; John Bulmer, London 54, 57 top right, 68, 74–5, 83, 89 top; Daily Telegraph Colour Library, London: John Hedgcoe 75 top, A. Howarth 41 bottom, Dmitri Kasterine 61 bottom; Bill Davidson, Penrith 32, 34–5 top and bottom, 40–1, 70–1, 71 top and bottom, 72–3, 78, 89 bottom, 90 top; Distillers Company, London 82; Hamlyn Group Picture Library 30 top, 60–1, 64 bottom; Robert Harding Associates, London 47; A. F. Kersting, London 12–13; Andrew Lawson, Oxford 10, 15 top and bottom, 16, 17 top and bottom, 41 top, 46 bottom, 61 top, 64 top, 65; Barry Lewis, London 56, 57 bottom; National Trust, London: Andy Williams 79; Mike Peters, London 21 upper right, 55, 62–3; Pix Photos, Aylesbury 66–7; Scottish Tourist Board, Edinburgh 84 left, 85 top right, 87 bottom, 91; Spectrum Colour Library, London 18, 20–1, 31, 33, 38, 39, 45 top and bottom, 46 top, 52 top, 58, 76 left, 90 bottom; Tony Stone Associates, London 11; Homer Sykes, London 21 bottom, 80 top, 81; Bob Thomlinson, Carlisle front endpapers, 30 bottom, 36 top, 43, 52–3 bottom, 53 top, 69, 73 bottom, 76 right, 86–7, 87 top, 88–9, 92; Wales Tourist Board, Cardiff: Harry Williams 50, Patrick Thurston 53 bottom right; ZEFA, London: J. Pfaff 22 bottom, F. Park 77.

The illustration on page 26 is reproduced by Gracious Permission of Her Majesty the Queen.

Remoteness and calm at Loch Tulla, near the Bridge of Orchy.